Together Everyone Achieves More -TEAM (work)

Various types of Lean and business improvement strategies (10x, RIO, Six Sigma, 5S, continual improvement models, etc.) employed across organizations teach and create the models for business excellence. Teamwork is often acknowledged as part of the correct mix for success in improvement oriented programs. In many business environments the word "teamwork" is thrown around to mean cooperation and corporate spirit among co-workers. A real need exists to define and understand the contribution of teamwork to the workplace with an eye toward the principles and goals teamwork embodies and sustains. Teamwork can be broken down into four simple elements and can provide a business asset when Together Everyone Achieves More- TEAM.

The first element of TEAM (work) is embodied in the word "together". Teams cannot operate at maximum capabilities and become proficient as sub-units functioning independently, or as individuals working assigned tasks without the group. Teams function together. Three key points measure the strength of the concept teamwork element "together": 1) Communication 2) Goal setting and progress measurements 3) Leadership assessment.

Communication is crucial to working together. Surprises, secrets, and holding back information are all symptoms of a team not functioning correctly. Within a team structure all members of the team should have access to the information and work of all other members of the team at any point in time. Flowing down communications is not conducive to a group structure and the circular transactional model of information flow needs to remain unbroken at all touch points.

Information is inserted at any one individual touch point in the group and creating a circular backward and forward flowing path of communication on the team ensures that there are never any "gaps" where individual teammates are not included. Goal setting and progress measurements determine the direction of the team and are useful in making sure that all team members continue to focus on the commonality of the intended goals. Individual efforts can sidetrack. Opinions on individual efforts and goal adjustments are frequent teamwork destroying factors. Objective measurements of project progress should be used such as: benchmarking, metrics assessments, and checklist scorecards. Re-defining goals, mid-project, based on measurements of progress is a team based exercise worth exploring, but teamwork goals should not form and change as a project evolves. Multiple goals are more effective than single objectives. With multiple goals, team resources can be continually in use rather than relying on phases of completion during which some team members work part of the time and remain idle the rest of the time. Leadership is necessary in any team format in order for coordination and cooperation of the team to be successful, although a teamwork leader may function as a facilitator more often than a director and should not be excluded from participating as a member of the team. Leadership qualities adapt to team needs. These qualities are not static and teams may rotate leadership roles based on the needs of the teamwork in progress. However, a leadership role must be respected as the force creating the glue in the project oversight or project flow capacity. Leadership assessments conducted by the team before and after new projects can pinpoint team leadership needs.

The second element of TEAM (work) can be found in the concept of "everyone". Individuals contribute to a team from their own skill sets and capabilities. Single tasks and group efforts are coordinated to work together to achieve the teamwork goals. Everything is done together by everyone on the team is not an efficient use of resources. Everyone contributes is crucial to teamwork success. Team resource allocation is a consideration of cost, time, physical assets, and information gathering or research that is best calculated by percentages of the total resource requirements at the beginning of a teamwork project. Putting together a teamwork project is akin to puzzle pieces fitting each other correctly for a perfect picture- all pieces are needed. Using the skill sets of each individual to benefit the team requires knowing the capabilities of each team member. Skills inventories and "training up" are useful applications that ensure "everyone" on a team is given the opportunity to deliver viable input. Developing and maximizing resource use includes all possible contributions.

"Achieve" is the third TEAM (work) element by which team success is measured. Goal setting is a common team exercise, but "achieving" is not simply declaring a purpose and accomplishing an end result. Achievement is measurable progress toward definitive improvements with the most efficient use of resources to obtain the desired outcome. Milestones, mid-project reviews and evaluations of the project in work, and cost/benefit analyses are tools that measure a team's capabilities to "achieve". It is not enough to produce an end result or to prove work in progress. When teamwork is functioning correctly measurable achievement produces goal attainment with successful results.

TEAM(work)

The fourth element of TEAM (work) requires the next-level progression found in the word "more". Teams are not static. If teamwork loses momentum, the team falls behind instead of sitting still. When people come together, "more" happens in teamwork dynamics than when individuals pursue their own efforts. Proof of momentum can be found in any group by assuring meeting minutes are noted and released and by notating action items promised and completed. Forward motion is not just achieving progress toward goals. Momentum results from solving complications, working out issues, and brainstorming new ideas. "More" from a team comes from individual inputs, group resolutions and co-operation, and stretching toward new developments.

Together Everyone Achieves More- TEAM (work)-is the conceptual model for group success. When the four elements of teamwork are defined and sustained, profits increase, return on investment (ROI) is improved, and Lean strategies are strengthened. Industries implementing team strategies should begin by establishing the TEAM concept. Team building exercises based on the TEAM framework elements optimize and sustain team growth. Goal oriented behaviors are supported when teams understand and embrace the TEAM functions and business excellence arises within the business environment.

- Kimberly Klemm

Together

Together Everyone Achieves More- TEAM (work) embodies the concept of "together" based on the idea of teaming. To understand the flow of teaming interactions, work structures must be evaluated. There are three roles within most work structure environments: 1) Those who do for others 2) Those who do and 3) Those who say what to do. This is a top down structure with those who say what to do at the top of the chain of command and those who do for others at the bottom. The concept of teaming simply stated is a group organized to work together. Confusion starts when any one functional element spans more than one work structure role. For example: To perform within a job at both the level of those who say what to do and those who do for others, it is necessary to show that the level of those who say what to do can be maintained while performing the tasks in the "those who do for others" category. Usually, we require these roles to remain separate in order not to cause confusion. On a team, these roles remain, but the concept of teaming teaches us that all individual roles contribute with equally valuable inputs for a team to be successful. In order to maintain balance while preserving structure, crossing roles within individual functions can provide stronger, more agile, and consistently productive teams.

To understand why this makes us uncomfortable, the concepts of "superior" and "inferior" have to be examined. The definition of superior states that superior is "something which is higher in a hierarchical structure". The definition of inferior is "lower in rank, status, or quality". To consider working together on a team requires status and quality to be a concept of the entire group. This leads to questioning the idea of arranging a team in a hierarchical structure as any sort of valid best practice. On the other hand confusion resulting from non-delineated roles causes failure as well.

Certain roles: team lead, team scribe, team treasurer, etc. have to be designated for team functions to be fulfilled. Often, such positions are rotated to maintain team status balances. Rotation schedules do not solve the issue of status balance because all individuals do not have the same capabilities and strengths. Constant overturn and fluctuation is not stabilization. Without team stabilization, productivity weakens. Crossing roles without eliminating functions creates a team without superior and inferior barriers. For example: In a treasurer's function, a team treasurer may be the one requested to collect dues in the role as one who does for the team; a team treasurer may also balance the accounts in the (autonomous role coupled with skill set function); and a team treasurer might be used in the role of one who says what to do over the money resource allocations (non-traditional treasurer role). All three levels are within the function of treasurer. The roles the treasurer performs cross a hierarchical structure's barriers, but the function (treasurer) is preserved. The perception of the value of the roles coupled with the perception of the value of the function creates a team perception of the value of the treasurer. When a team evaluates its performance, value added or non-value added designations are made in the effort to create efficiency and greater return on investment (ROI). However, when evaluating a team "togetherness" asking about value added or non-value added functions involves the perception or roles as well as the question of function productivity.

The Lean concept of Gemba walks was born from the idea that those atop a hierarchical structure would "come down" from the higher functions and observe the environments and work of those at "lower levels"- later this broadened to all level functions taking walks together to closely observe arenas not familiar within the productive functions. Widening knowledge and understanding of the functions and roles of others and looking with "new eyes" at familiar structured work environments became a key point to successful Gemba walks.

The process of level setting skills and tasks is part of determining how to best use team roles to cross structurally within stable functions. Balancing high and low level skills is necessary for team stability. On the other hand, teams are not in balance when certain functions or individuals are labeled "high" or "low". To cross the hierarchical boundaries, each stable team function should be built on "high", "low", and "neutral" roles to create equality and respect between individual teammates. This is why skills and tasks must be level set. Lower level sets on skills might be counterbalanced by higher-level tasks. High skill level sets do not necessarily equal high-level tasks. It might take a very high level set skill to precisely build the interior of a watch. Building the interior of a watch might be a common factor level assembly job (even if the assembly is performed by one person). A less skilled act is creating an advertisement for the watch to sell. The task of creating the advertisement is probably an office level set task with more decision power involved in the fate of the watch. This is actually a balance. High-level skills must perform high-level tasks and low-level skills must perform low level tasks is an upset on the balance of every individual contribution respected. The watchmaker will not usually create great advertising and the advertising executive usually cannot build a watch as well. An approach to level setting has been given in the past for cross-training everyone to be capable of everyone else's function. This eliminates stable functions by the "cog and wheel" replacement is easy idea. Teammates are not valued in this ideology; all are simply replaceable parts. To stabilize a team and create a "together" concept, each function needed on the team must be represented by the individual filling that function. Level sets of skills and tasks can be used to establish roles within stable functions that cross the "high"/"low" boundary concept of hierarchical thinking.

Exercise A.1.a

Cut strings in progressively shorter lengths and lay them out in a pyramid with the longest string on the bottom progressively narrowing toward the shortest string on the top. Break the group into two or three teams.

Each team will be assigned a different shape to form from the strings (square, circle, or rectangle). There can be no discussion of how to form the shape or what to do with the strings within each team when it is their turn. ALL strings must be included in the shape and every string must touch another string on both ends. Each team may work as long as they like. However, if any one teammate calls out "Finished" the team effort is over and someone on the team must announce: "Finished" before the team can sit down.

Take pictures of each teams effort and vote on the "best" shape as an entire group.

The purpose of this exercise is to show that communication about the properties of each string and how to use each string would benefit a team effort to accomplish building their shape. Team members are not given individual roles or tasks and everyone is to contribute. Together is not established. If a team is successful and everyone on the team contributes and works together, there are still not valid function structures and direction is tacit agreement.

Open a discussion on the results and what it feels like to perform this exercise in relation to the TEAM(work) concept "Together".

Pulling Together- Criticism and Development

TEAM(work) requires a team that not only functions well together, but teammates that develop in the same direction. Development requires 1) learning 2) evaluation and 3) implementation of new methods, principles and ideas. Various business models exist for development within the team structure. Examples of business culture learning models are: Lean, Agile, ESSO, etc.

Learning for development can take place in several ways including traditional teaching training, OJT, and gradual integration. Before the effectiveness of any new development initiative can be assessed, the learning stage must be completed. Often, when a team first forms, there is some sort of learning necessary before the team can perform their goal functions adequately. Team assessments should never occur at the beginning of the development cycle. The learning stage of development is not static as a placeholder for new teams or new team members. Whenever a team must restructure or embrace a different structural development, the learning stage will begin again. Examples of this type of learning reoccurrence can be found when a team starts a different project or when the goals for a team are rewritten. While different development methods may be employed across various industries, within the basic structures the weakest part of team development occurs during the evaluation stage. Evaluation is used to check on progress, discover problems occurring, and offer an opportunity for greater input from teammates. Regardless of development systems or methods, a team must adapt to criticism in evaluation as some form of a healthy exercise instead of a negative and separating endeavor. As human beings, we find automatic defensiveness against negative factors and can be embarrassed if our contributions are lessened in the eyes of those we choose to need respect from. Teammates necessarily must respect each other to work well together. Some of the stress of the evaluative cycle can be relieved by individual responsibility for self-critique and independent reporting. This requires coordination of each individual input into a picture for the team framework and the overall goal alignment. Working on the coordination of individual evaluative inputs produces the best results when the entire team is aware of the input information and has a chance to give feedback, as a team together, on the coordination of evaluations into the team's development. Implementing self-critiques and reporting does not mean that teammates and leaders should refrain from input on weaknesses. Feedback is crucial in the evaluation stage. Feedback incorporates others within the TEAM(work) structure and creates a link that establishes that individual evaluation is an integrated piece of the team's functionality, not a freedom to be separate from the team structure.

It is also human nature to justify weaknesses. Valid justifications that only rely on information should be allowable. Informative justifications can be used as a starting point to find accurate root causes and requirements for adaptations of processes. Justifications that switch focus to the work or behaviors of other teammates are not valid. Other teammates should not be used for diversions as problem identifications or solutions. These types of justifications are divisive and will affect the capability of a team to work "Together" on both personal and professional levels. Other teammates should be mentioned for any part they have actually contributed to the information.

In every evaluation cycle, honesty is a crucial element. If honesty is not upheld during the evaluation stage the team structure will fail and the image of the team will weaken. Process points, resource requirements, progress analysis and material data are necessary pieces of information to obtain when a self-critique or other type of evaluation shows a problem. Criticism constructively used creates stronger implementation of new methods, principles and ideas.

The implementation of new methods, principles and ideas is the final stage of development. This occurs after learning and evaluation as the application of a competent introduction of the method, principle or idea into the working environment. Implementation stages are sometimes referred to as performance cycles. An implementation stage is often followed by a review. Reviews are not equivalent to evaluations. Reviews are intended to measure performance. Evaluations are created to assess strengths and weaknesses to adjust models, methods and principles before the implementation stage.

Teams must implement methods, principles and ideas "Together". This is why the first stages of learning and evaluation are critical to forming confidence on a team. Teaming comes together in learning and evaluation, but the test of successful team building occurs when team building turns into team structure. The structure of team functions and the responsibility of team function roles will sustain implementation under performance measurements or the process of team building has not accomplished the goals.

The implementation stage of development is where the "work" in TEAM(work) occurs. Implementation is not the beginning of new methods, principles and ideas.

Instead, implementation is the "Goal" stage where learning, planning, and evaluation are finished and work ensues in the PDCA cycle before a performance review is conducted. By the time implementation starts, team goals are already achieved or the final steps to goal attainment are in progress. In implementation a finished model or methodology is asked to produce results. Including productivity in team goals requires an external base other than teaming successfully to measure contribution. Even if teammates are the only workers affected by an implementation, the implementation measurements and defining criteria of implementation application fall into the "work" part of TEAM(work) and are usually not equivalent to the same ideologies used to create TEAM concepts and functions. However, if a team is successful, the TEAM concepts and functions will carry over to the "work" of the implementation stage and will pull the first lessons of "Together" to benefit the work at hand.

Exercise A.1.b

All members of the group are told they are going to conduct an evaluation of each other's attire. Critiques must be limited to clothing only. Every group member is given an option: the group may critique their attire or they may conduct a critique of their own attire in front of the group. All group members will participate.

Line the room with large sheets of white paper on the wall and use a magic marker to write down every comment of each individual critique. When the evaluations are through, state that invalid comments will now be crossed off all of the white sheets of paper. Strike-through every subjective comment that is not purely factual as invalid.

The purpose of this exercise is to show that valid evaluations are based on factual information and that personal criticism is invalid as an evaluation.

Ask the group members to discuss the differences in how it felt to be critiqued by the group as opposed to the experiences of those who performed self-critiques. Inquire how group members felt about other group members that participated by choosing differently in how to be critiqued than their own decision.

Achieve

For a team to achieve their purpose by attaining goals there are three key elements that are employed: Communication, Empowerment, and Implementation. Communication is the vehicle or tool for attaining achievements and effective communication increases the capability of the team to work together supporting each individual effort. Knowledge and interpretation are the cornerstones of communication. Within a team structure there are three types of knowledge: 1) collective knowledge 2) individual knowledge and 3) external knowledge. Collective knowledge is the knowledge of the team together from everyone. When individual knowledge is contributed to collective knowledge the collective knowledge grows. However, collective knowledge is not just the sum of individual knowledge pieces. As individual knowledge is added to collective knowledge, ideas, facts and information that are not apparent without putting together individual knowledge pieces become clear. If team knowledge is not collective knowledge, part of the reservoir of information will not be attainable.

Individual knowledge must remain the property of the individual. This is another reason that teams require "everyone". To properly equip collective knowledge, individual knowledge is contributed but it reposes within the individuals of the team. Teams use knowledge collectively, they do not own knowledge collectively. Losing teammates hurts the collective knowledge of the team largely due to individual knowledge ownership residing in interpretive capability.

Communication of individuals in the team framework requires a trust factor. Secrecy of individual knowledge in an effort to retain position or status hurts the function of collective knowledge. Understanding of the roles of both individual knowledge and collective knowledge is a beginning point of valuation of every teammate that results in team strength to communicate clearly and openly for the greater benefit of collective knowledge.

External knowledge comes from sources outside of the team and may be brought to the collective knowledge base by individuals, but external knowledge should not be portrayed as individual knowledge. "Cite the source," is an old newspaper adage that is very applicable to external knowledge designations. External knowledge benefits individual knowledge when individual knowledge is increased by further insight, learning, or work performed in addition to the original input from an external knowledge source. This is similar to how individual knowledge contributes to collective knowledge.

Interpretation adds to, detracts from, or renews any of the three types of knowledge. External knowledge becomes individual knowledge when interpretation changes the scope, use, or understanding of the external knowledge. Individual knowledge becomes collective knowledge when it is added to the team's knowledge as a group and the group's interpretation as a whole can perform the same function of information transformation. Even though this information transformation makes the knowledge "More", interpretation can detract from the knowledge by pointing up inconsistencies, inadequacies, and misinformation within the knowledge. This does not mean that the detracted knowledge is less. The detracted knowledge is still "More" due to interpretation that could not be added without the transfer from external knowledge to individual knowledge or the transfer from individual knowledge to collective knowledge. Knowledge that is discounted as trivial or irrelevant can be renewed as viable by interpretation in information transformation. Communication is used to effect the creation of a team collective knowledge and to clearly transfer interpretations.

There are numerous communication models and methods. Regardless of how communication is conducted, the purpose of communication is to relay information. On a team, single point-to-point communications are not a realistic picture of a comprehensive communication strategy. Teams that collaborate only one-on-one do not interact as a group and cannot be included under the concept of teaming found in this book. Singular input points to the communication hubs and to individual teammates are required for team interaction. On the other hand, singular inputs cannot be the only communication interaction points to support team needs. Collective input methods are still required for good team communication. A collective input can result from a group repository on-line, face-to-face all teammate meetings, or distributions in print of all singular input communications put together to be read at once. This is due to the interpretation transformation of information when it is presented collectively.

There is a myth that only team leads and team managers need a collective overview. This myth is based on the mentality that only leadership interpretations add to the collective knowledge on the team. Interpretation is a didactic vehicle; it is interpersonal. When only team leadership is allowed interpersonal communication interpretation, the collective team knowledge suffers from isolating interpersonal growth as a top down answer instead of acknowledging the growth of knowledge nourishing each other in the garden bed of the team that could bring forth a more plentiful harvest. This does not mean that leadership is not needed for direction.

Exercise A.3.a

This is an example pointing to the capabilities of leadership to explore possibilities:

1. Write on the blackboard the numbers 1, 2, and 3 (no commas).
2. Ask the group to interpret the meaning of what is on the blackboard.
3. Warn the group that if everyone gives the same answer, the group fails.
4. Tell the group that the group has to agree on an answer about the interpretation of the numbers.

The interpretation is 1, 2, and 3 can be many things. For example: one hundred and twenty three, or one count repeated three times, or the number six, etc.

If everyone knows the correct answer and there is total group agreement, then the group does not think of more than one possibility in a given situation. If there are several answers, and the group can state different answers, then decisions can be a team effort without the fault of not considering alternatives. If the group has individuals that state answers in the face of group agreement, then the group has individuals that can stand up to criticism and still contribute.

A discussion after the group decides on an answer should point to the fact that both individuality and TEAM(work) are necessary characteristics on a team. Effective leadership can direct the group to find an answer, but not answer for the group without discounting interpretations that open other possibilities.

Empowerment

Empowerment is a decision. The vehicle of communication enables teammates to embrace empowerment to achieve goals. Empowerment is not the capability to have control over others; it is not a decision that includes some teammates and excludes other teammates. If a team is not empowered together, then the concept of empowerment becomes the struggle for power and position instead of a force that equips everyone to achieve.

The decision to empower a team must originate in team leadership and team supports. Empowerment can come from sources external to the team as well as from within the team structure. Empowerment can be given and empowerment can be taken away, but it is not to be confused with decision-making capabilities. Decisions are not the result of true empowerment; empowerment is a decision. When initiative is supported, decisions become more informed, creative, and achieve greater impacts in results. Teams are not empowered to give certain answers or decisions or to deliver expected achievements. The mindset of "empowered to perform" creates a misconception that empowerment is the bestowing and removal of positions.

Initiative is the cornerstone of empowerment. This is why a top down empowerment does not tap into the synergy of the team to create progress toward the team's purpose. As team communication creates a collective knowledge and the benefit of individual interpretations add to team communication, a team must have the drive of initiative to succeed in achievements. Team leadership that drives on strong initiative should seek to foster individual and collective initiative within teammates. There should not be a forbidden aspect to putting ideas forward or working toward team achievements. At times, the functions of a teammate may expand in scope due to individual initiatives. This should not be discouraged, but the work and results should be included through team communication to produce a collective initiative that involves other teammates.

The concept of ownership threatens empowerment on a team and individual level. To begin an initiative individually requires taking ownership of the initiative. Incorporating an individual initiative into the team's collective initiative becomes a question of ownership. When a team embraces an individual initiative as common property, the initiative becomes collective and the team is empowered. If a team does NOT embrace and own an individual initiative, the individual can be seen as a threat to the TEAM(work) environment or as disassociated from other teammates. Team leadership can mediate this effect by contributing support at the individual initiative levels.

To empower a team there must be an environment that fosters open communication, acceptance, trust, and the concept of "Together". The breakdown of these factors in a team's environment disintegrates the empowerment decision. Individual initiatives must be communicated back to the team for possible integration into collective initiatives. In an environment where communication is not openly received and accepted, information will not be returned to add to the team collective and the capability of achieving more will be reduced. When teammates are overly concerned with position and team trust is eroded through competition, a team is no longer functioning "Together" and individual initiative is seen as an advantage over teammates, not as an empowered capability that should contribute back to the team.

Teammates' functions in their prescribed roles on the team are crucial key points of responsibility within team structure that need to be upheld. This does NOT mean that initiative should be discouraged unless it fits prescribed boundaries. When team leadership establishes team goals to fulfill the team's purpose, if team goals are prescribed and initiative is discouraged- the only achievements the team will attain are achievements already planned. Empowerment allows a team to achieve and reach toward more than just what is demanded and expected as a result of set outcomes. TEAM(work) encourages empowerment in order to increase the potential of synergies occurring by incorporating the full worth of individual contributions into a collective greater exponential factor.

It can be argued that attaining goals is not the same as achieving progress. To attain a goal, a runner arrives at the finish line. To achieve progress, a runner arrives at the finish line in better time than he finished the last race. In a relay race each runner completing their leg of the race with an individual better time contributes to their team finishing faster even though only one runner will cross the finish line. Team goals should not be set to attain. Team goals should be set to achieve. Attainment goals outline role function responsibilities and their completion expectations. Achievement goals create more in their description than role function items. It is beneficial to team empowerment to enlist the entire team in goal setting intended to fulfill the team's purpose. There is a section in the next chapter on "Goal Setting".

Empowerment comes from others not from the individual self. By its very definition, empowerment is an external force working for internal achievement. Individuals can be self-motivated, self-directing, and self-sustaining but empowerment is given by others to support these self-oriented characteristics and to bring them into focus as valuable to the team where teammates can add to and build on individual pursuits. Empower individuals and empower their team; empower a team and achieve instead of attain.

TEAM(work)

Exercise A.3.b

Group Hug Modification Exercise

The Group Hug has long been a symbol of acceptance and togetherness. This exercise is meant to show how the environment of open communication, acceptance, trust, and the concept of "Together" can lend individuals a sense of empowerment and how choices are made on an individual level that can exclude others from this feeling of empowerment.

1. Everyone in the group must hug three people and no more than three people.
2. If someone hugs an individual, this does not qualify as a hug for the "hugee" as well as the "hugger". Roles must be stated ahead of the hug. (Example: "I am hugging you," means someone is the hugger not the huggee.)
3. One person at a time chooses those that they will hug.

Three things must happen for the group to succeed at this exercise:

1. Everyone must receive a hug as a huggee from a hugger.
2. No one member of the group should receive an inordinate number of hugs.
3. There should be no refusals to "hug next".

After all group members have had an opportunity to be the hugger discuss these points:

- Was anyone left out?
- Was anyone unwilling to step up as a hugger?
- Is popularity a factor in being a huggee?

- How is cognizance of position and inclusion a part of acceptance?

Include the three success points as criteria the group was unaware of and ask for feedback on the group decision of failure or success.

Implementation of Initiative (Organization and Progress)

The implementation of initiative requires embracing the empowerment decision through the vehicle of communication to achieve team goals. On the other hand, implementation is more than acceptance of a route for progress. Effective implementation applies organization to structure, clarify, and resource progress decisions through quantification and records keeping. This enhances and supports the momentum of initiative.

Organization costs time and resources that, if properly allocated, will feed into the profitability of the total return of investment achieved by implementing team initiative and accomplishing team goals. Allocating resources and time for organization should not be a haphazard endeavor. Part of incorporating organization into a team structure to assist with initiative implementations is planning the organization needs, methods, and tools. Organization planning is NOT separate from the concept of organization; it is part of the concept of organization. The percentage of time and resources allotted for organization methods and tools to be implemented should also include time and resources for planning organization. Without some form of organization, progress is a "hit and miss" target practice composed only of skill, environment, and chance. Progress that relies on skill, environment, and chance cannot always move forward. Organization paves a path toward a goal and keeps the initiative vehicles "on the road". Communication and empowerment are enabled by the methods and tools of organization and will become impossible to manage without an organized structure to support the team needs in these cornerstones of achievement.

Although organization methods and tools are vital to achieving team progress, goal achievement measurements should not include organizational accomplishments or organizational benchmarks as part of the assessment of achievement progress. Organization is a catalyst enabling achievement. Since progress is marked by advancement toward a goal, organization does not mark progress because, on its own, organization is not advancement. This does not mean that organization is not necessary for advancements. The exception to this rule is created when a goal is in and of itself an organizational goal.

Once a team has established communication, empowered teammates, and organized for forward motion, a team can then implement the initiative to achieve progress. An initiative statement can be created in order to clarify the work toward team purpose attainment. Initiative statements are only one to three sentences long and should not contain passive language. They can incorporate a re-statement of team goals. On the other hand, an initiative statement is not a goal statement. An initiative statement includes the procedure or procedures that will be followed toward goal attainment and can include the milestones that will be used to benchmark progress. Some teams will prefer to create an initiative plan documenting the entire process toward achievement. An initiative plan should still have one or two sentences as a stand-alone initiative statement that completely encapsulates implementation intentions. Initiative plans show the procedure plans, not the explicit work instructions.

Examples of the differences between goal statements; initiative statement; initiative plans; work instructions are below:

Goal statement: This team will achieve the reinforcement of the bottom of the broken chair in our meeting room.

Initiative statement: This team will place boards across the bottom of the broken chair in our meeting room and use nails to secure the reinforcement in order to repair the broken chair seat.

Initiative plan (might include): Obtain three nails, a hammer, and two boards; place the boards across the bottom of the broken seat; hammer the three nails into the middle of the boards. (Process steps)

Work instructions (might include): Hold a carpenter's hammer in the left or right hand. Grip the hammer handle firmly and close the left or right hand around it. Place a flat-head nail ¾' diameter and ¼" long halfway up the board with the pointed side down. Strike the nail head at a sixty-degree angle with the hammer. Implementation of the initiative statement and an initiative plan will require continual embracement of empowerment for decision-making and the vehicle of communication to support and sustain organization. While a team's purpose may exist from the beginning creation of a team, before an initiative statement is constructed team roles and functions have to be established.

Team roles and team functions can be static or rotational during the lifetime of the team. On the other hand, team roles and team functions are not arbitrary and should only be designated once the needs for particular roles and functions are determined. Due to the fact that team needs change during the different phases of a team project, team needs will dictate that some team roles and functions are temporary in nature. This should not be an excuse to eliminate team members or to add excessive teammate additions once the team is established. Constantly rotating team membership destroys the cohesive nature of teaming together and limits the team's capability to achieve. Every time a team chooses a new purpose, sets new team goals, or loses a teammate re-teaming is recommended. There is a discussion on re-teaming in the "Work" section of this book.

TEAM(work)

Exercise A.3.c

Bring three sets (boxes) of 100 toothpicks to the group. Have the group divide into three teams, counting off around the room "1". "2", "3", "1","2","3", etc. until everyone has a number from one to three and then split the teams by similar numbered designations.

<u>Instructions to Team 1</u>: Open the box of toothpicks. Separate the toothpicks into individual piles of five toothpicks each and deliver a viable count of how many toothpicks you have been given.

<u>Instructions to Team 2:</u> Count the number of toothpicks in the box. Do NOT divide the toothpicks into smaller individual groups of toothpicks.

<u>Instructions to Team 3:</u> (Dump Team 3's toothpicks out of the box into a pile). DO NOT touch the toothpicks. DO still count all of the toothpicks.

Wait up to a half hour for the teams to finish the exercise. Then call time if the teams are not finished.

1. Which Team finished first? Did organizational capabilities contribute to this factor?
2. Was there any frustration in teammates on any of the teams?
3. Did Team 2 come up with a better way to count toothpicks? How does standardization apply to this task?
4. Was this task easy or hard and unfair?
5. Did everyone finish the task within the time frame?

More
Exercises for this module are optional and not tied to the content of this section. Optional Exercises are found in the Appendix for Optional Exercises at the end of the book.

"More" is just that: more of any resource, effort or return on investment (ROI); surpassing goal expectations; increased percentages in analytics, etc. When examining the concept of "More" two target areas, Purposing and Goal Setting, focus realization of how TEAM(work) produces better results than efforts that do not encompass the ideologies inherent in "**T**ogether **E**veryone **A**chieves **M**ore". Purposing for a team is more than setting the goals to achieve. When a goal is created for a business purpose, there is an expected ROI. Resources can be replenished and renewed at higher levels from a goal attainment without ever producing any actual return independent of resource reinvestment. This is indicative of false ROI because the resource renewal did not create a measurable element of return, as resources are simple investment capital and sustaining or improving investment capital is not the same as showing a profit. Goals that do not create a business need met AND produce a return on the resource investment required need to be evaluated for sustainability. Business needs usually require a business case preparation that will show the ROI is applicable as actual profit to the business entity. Also, ROI is relative within the concept of "More". For example: Ten cents invested in an opportunity that creates a net profit does NOT return as much as ten dollars invested in the same opportunity. Technically the ROI is the same on both investments. In hard reality the ten dollars made more. These principles of needs met/return on resources and ROI relativity must be included when evaluation team goals. Purposing should encompass team skill, team resources, and an effort expectancy index.

Effort expectancy indexes can be created from measuring time requirements, productivity norms, and percentages of input required from each team members contributions to achieve goal attainments. (See the tables below for formula inputs and outputs examples creating an expectancy index.)

Table 1. Time Requirement Index

Time Requirements	Expected Time to Complete	Acceptable Delay	Time Compensation Allowable	Final Time Requirement Index Number
60 minutes	60 minutes	30 minutes	15 minutes	(60 minutes minus 30 minutes plus 15 minutes) **75 minutes total**

To gain a Final Time Requirement Index number:

1) Determine the time requirement allotted for the work. This usually comes from planning and deciding how much time can be scheduled within the workload for the project.

2) Determine the EXPECTED time it will take to complete the work required. This is different than the allowed time scheduled and derives an input from the workers assessment of what it will take to actually perform the workload.

3) Build in an acceptable delay time. When planning determines the amount of time that can be allowed for a project, there should also be estimation available of how late the project results can be produced if they are not delivered on time and still fit within an acceptable window.

4) Figure on a realistic time compensation for errors, problems, or delays that are unforeseen.

The formula for Table 1. is:

Expected Time to Complete – (minus) Acceptable Delay + (plus) Time Compensation Allowable = (equals) Final Time Requirement Index Number.

The Final Time Requirement Index Number should be compared to the original Time Requirements Number as an assessment of the actual time resource needed from each individual on the project (in this case 75 minutes per individual) to finish the project. If the gap between the Final Time Requirement Index Number and Time Requirements Number is too large, project sustainability should be questioned (before investing or attempting a project). In the table above with the figures provided this is an acceptable investment as a project under the Final Time Requirement because the Final Time Requirement Index Number is below the figure obtained when adding the Expected Time to Complete with the Acceptable Delay. If the Time Compensation Allowable is greater than the Acceptable Delay, the percentage of overage in the Final Time Requirement Index Number must fall within 50% of the original Time Requirements figure to be considered as a sustainable time resource commitment.

The Time Requirement Index is necessary as a tool for deciding on the viability of a project before it is subsidized. To establish a project, the purpose of the project must be sustainable. As a preliminary exercise, the Time Requirement Index indicates workload commitment that can or cannot be supported within the scope of a project. Although this might not seem like purposing, a project is created for a reason and results. The reason and results of a project are the purpose for undertaking an endeavor. If the reason for a project is viable and resources for results are not realistically obtainable, then the purpose of the project is faulted. For this reason, when the principles of empowerment and communication are in action on a team and teammates work "Together" the resources available for purposing become "More" than just the time a team can commit to a project by team meetings and work done only as a group. Working out the total time commitments required of all team mates combined for the project is addressed in the Resource Commitments Index in Table 3. under the Time Available column. The reason this figure is not included in the Time Requirement Index is that the Time Requirement Index Is built to address individual workloads so that a team project assessment can take every team mates individual capacities into consideration before pitching a project. The Final Time Requirement Index Number is an indication of team mate project resource capacities from each team mate's workload perspective and can be used to scope the entire team project as a standard estimate or teams can apply this index to individual prospects of inclusion within a proposed team project.

The Productivity Norm Index (See Table 2. below) is dependent on three separate formulated steps and arrives at the Final Productivity Norm Index Number through a series of calculations producing the Units Produced per Designated Time Unit, the Most Frequent Shortage of Units per Norm of Time Unit, and the Final Productivity Norm Index Number. The designation of "units" is an arbitrary term and can represent any unitized measurable output of work. The Productivity Norm Index is useful for projects that have already been started as a measure of sustainability. The Final Productivity Norm Index Number will not be greater than the stated Productivity Norms for a sustainable workload without increasing resources.

Table 2. Productivity Norm Index

Productivity Norms	Units Produced per Designated Time Unit	Most Frequent Shortage of Units per Norm of Time Unit	Overproduction Capacity	Final Productivity Norm Index Number
15 Units	1.25 hours (Final Time Requirement Index Number) (+) plus 15 (Productivity Norm Figure) (1.25 + 15 = 16.25) (÷) divided by 2 (Number of Time Requirements Units) (16.25 ÷ 2 = 8.75) **8.75 (Units Produced per Designated Time Unit)**	Shortage = 15 (Productivity Norm) (-) minus 8.75 Units Produced per Designated Time Unit (15-8.75= 6.25) (÷) divided by 2 (Number of Time Requirements Units) (6.25 ÷ 2= 3.125) Rounded to the nearest whole number **3 Units (Most Frequent Shortage of Units per Norm of Time Unit)**	2 Units	8.75 (Units Produced per Designated Time Unit) (+) plus 3 (Most Frequent Shortage of Units per Norm of Time Unit) (8.75 + 3 = 11.75) (-) minus 2 (Overproduction Capacity) (11.75 - 2= 9.75) Rounded to the nearest whole number **10 (Final Productivity Norm Index Number)**

The Productivity Norms column reflects the units of output per time unit (found in the Time Requirements designation of the Time Requirement Index) currently actually produced on average. The Units Produced per Designated Time Units figure reflects the Productivity Norm that occurs within the time allotment of the Final Time Requirement Index Number's allowance, given this formula:

Final Time Requirement Index Number + (plus) Productivity Norm ÷ (divided by) Total Number of Time Requirements Units required (as a whole number- round up) to complete the time incorporated by the Final Time Requirement Index Number = (equals) Units Produced by Designated Time Units

In the example above the Units Produced by Designated Time Units is a number less than the Productivity Norm. This indicates that according to the Final Time Requirement Index the project is NOT overburdening production capacities to continue to achieve project goals within the budgeted time allowed. If the Units Produced by Designated Time Units showed a number greater than the Productivity Norm, there would be reason to believe that work on the project was not being accomplished.

The Most Frequent Shortage of Units per Norm of Time Unit is a determination of the average shortage occurring within the project scope of the time spent on the designated project. This is not the same number as the average shortage expected for the Productivity Norm.

The formula for The Most Frequent Shortage of Units per Norm of Time Unit is given as:

Productivity Norm – (minus) Units Produced per Designated Time Units ÷ (divided by) Number of Time Requirements Units = (equals) The Most Frequent Shortage of Units per Norm of Time Unit (always rounded to the nearest whole number).

Because the Units Produced per Designated Time Units should be less than or equal to the Productivity Norm, the difference pinpoints the loss of productivity to the work statement that is acceptable for the scope of the project. The Number of Time Requirements Units must be factored as a divisor to scale this number to measurable project time units designated for project endeavors. The Most Frequent Shortage of Units per Norm of Time Unit is rounded to the nearest whole number because there is theoretically not a way to produce a partial "unit" (however unit of work has been determined) as output. This column is not an indicator number of project sustainability, rather the number of the Most Frequent Shortage of Units per Norm of Time Unit is intended as a measure against actual units produced. There should not be an occurrence of the number of actual work units produced falling below the acceptable shortage reflected by the Most Frequent Shortage of Units per Norm of Time Unit without flagging actual production as stalled.

In the Overproduction Capacity column, the number should be entered from knowledge of the number of units that can be produced without straining the capability of facilities and resources to sustain in overproduction. The Overproduction Capacity number is not calculated on the table.

If the number for Overproduction Capacity is NOT available, make a best guess and use a number equal to or less than the Most Frequent Shortage of Units per Norm of Time Unit figure.

The Final Productivity Norm Index Number is the sum total, on a scale of one to twenty, of a scale reflecting the rating of the productivity of the project factoring in production norms, shortages, and overage. The formula is as follows:

Units Produced per Designated Time Units + (plus) Most Frequent Shortage of Units per Norm of Time Unit – (minus) Overproduction Capacity = (equals) Final Productivity Norm Index Number (always rounded to the nearest whole number)

Units Produced per Designated Time Units are added to Most Frequent Shortage of Units per Norm of Time Unit to determine how many units will be needed to make up for shortages. Overproduction Capacity is subtracted from this number to stabilize the productivity expected to make up for shortages. (Overage does not count when adjusting for a shortage.) The final number is the Final Productivity Norm Index Number and this is always rounded to a whole number for assessment on the Productivity Index Scale (1-20). Any project that has a Final Productivity Norm Index Number falling between the numbers one and ten on the Productivity Index Scale is sustaining its purpose through productive work. Projects that have a Final Productivity Norm Index Number falling between fifteen and twenty on the Productivity Index Scale need reevaluation at the purposing level as the original intent of the project is not finding workable, supportive productivity levels.

Purpose is not something determined at the beginning of a team project and not reevaluated throughout the entire team endeavor.

The Productivity Norm Index is an effort index that can be used, once a team project is launched, to determine resource/workload sustainability. Using the Productivity Norm Index is still a part of team purposing because it can support, deny, or indicate adjustments needed for the premise of the Time Requirement Index that a team project is or is not an endeavor or purpose that will achieve its goals. With the Productivity Norm Index, a team can work out sustainable productivity levels and reach toward "More" through workload distribution adjustments and re-evaluation of goals and targets. The TEAM(work) principles of "Together Everyone" make productivity analysis a shared burden, not an individually targeted review of a team mate's statement of work. To surpass team goal expectations resources have to be properly managed. The Productivity Norm Index can be used as a tool to guide team resource decisions.

The Resource Commitments Index (See Table 3. below) shows several factors that can be used in determining resource needs at a project start or for teams tracking resource adjustments needed for projects in progress. Individual resource needs are not itemized. The Resource Commitments Index addresses effort expectancies and time/effort indications. Team mate contributions from their efforts will vary in type and requirements, but an effort expectancy measurement can indicate team functionality expectations under a project workload and pinpoint team project endeavor distribution needs among team mates to keep a balanced, on target project that involves "Everyone".

Table 3. Resource Commitments Index

Percentage of Individual Input Required	Time Available	Individual Resources Weighted Contribution	Percentage of Workload Needing Over Average Contribution	Final Outside Team Resource Commitments Needed
100 % ÷ (divided by) Number of Team Members (for this example 5) = (equals) 20% (100% ÷ 5 = 20%)	75 minutes (Final Time Requirement Index Number) x (multiplied by) Number of Team Members (5) = (equals) 6.25 hours (1.23 x 5= 6.25)	20% x (multiplied by) Time Available (6.25) = (equals) 1.25 (20% x 6.25= 1.25) weighted for distribution by dividing by (÷) 5 (Number of Team Members) = (equals) 25% (1.25 ÷ 5= 25%)	100% - (minus) 25% (Individual Resources Weighted Contribution) = (equals) 75% (100%-25%= 75%)	75% (Percentage of Workload Needing Over Average Contribution) - (minus) 20% (Percentage of Individual Input Required) = (equals) 55% (75%-20%= 55%)

Percentage of Individual Input Required is a simple measurement based on an expected effort of 100% from all teammates combined. The Number of Team Members is used as a divisor for the total expected effort of 100% because in theory, workloads should be distributed evenly among all team members.

Time Available is the duration of time each team member should be committing to the project for 100% effort. The formula for the Time Available column is:

Final Time Requirement Index Number x (multiplied by) Number of Team Members = (equals) Hours needed from each team member for team project to be expending 100% effort.

Individual Resources Weighted Contribution measures Time Available against Percentage of Individual Input Required and arrives at a weighted contribution that determines the amount of ACTUAL percentage of effort needed from each team member to complete the project within the project Final Time Requirement applied across all team member workloads. To arrive at the Individual Resources Weighted Contribution follow this formula:

Percentage of Individual Input Required x (multiplied by) Time Available ÷ (divided by) Number of Team Members = (equals) Individual Resources Weighted Contribution

The Percentage of Workload Needing Over Average Contribution shows the percentage of extra team effort required from the entire team as measured against the complete team project (100%) and is arrived at with the formula below:

Work on project complete when project is finished (always theoretically based as 100%) – (minus) Individual Resources Weighted Contribution = (equals) Percentage of Workload Needing Over Average Contribution

Removal of the Individual Resources Weighted Contribution figure eliminates the workload of one team member and the additional work that is shown required by the Individual Resources Weighted Contribution percentage number. This arrives at the Percentage of Workload Needing Over Average Contribution as a percentage reflecting not only the extra effort required reflected in the Individual Resources Weighted Contribution, but also factoring for performance levels variations that realistically will not always sustain goal levels for individual workloads. Basing this, representatively, on one team mate's contributions NOT functioning is the equivalent to losing one person on the team. If the workload of the entire team suffers degradation across all team mates, a project can still be sustained as long as the entire effort degradation is not lower than the total effort input required for the project from a single team mate. The Percentage of Workload Needing Over Average Contribution is a "worst case" percentage figure allowing for a target range of effort expectancy that has a high margin of return if team performance degradation is less than the maximum accepted loss of effort from one entire team member's contribution and loss, as well, of the extra effort needed from that team mate. This is not a percentage measured on actual performance. The percentage is derived from effort loss expectancy.

The example above shows the Percentage of Workload Needing Over Average Contribution as 75%. If the Percentage of Workload Needing Over Average Contribution is more than the Individual Resources Weighted Contribution, added to the Individual Resources Weighted Contribution, there are not enough team members involved in the project to pull the workload from the outset of the project. This column can be used to assess the risk factor in allotting team project resources. While it shows the percentage required for resource recovery during project upset or failure, the Percentage of Workload Needing Over Average Contribution cannot be used as a direct measurement of the team project.

To arrive at the Final Outside Team Resource Commitments Needed percentage, the Percentage of Individual Input Required is subtracted from the Percentage of Workload Needing Over Average Contribution. The column for Final Outside Team Resource Commitments Needed is a measurement that reflects the percentage of work effort needed to sustain average work shortages and achieve "More" than just the required minimum of meeting team project goals. To achieve "More" is interpreted as obtaining an ROI, not just breaking even on input/output configurations. The workload for one team mate's Percentage of Individual Input Required is added back in (without the weighted contribution) to stabilize the worst case scenario from the Percentage of Workload Needing Over Average Contribution and this calculation gives the over-average percentage required from each team member's expected workload average to achieve "More" than the bare minimum required by the project scope. The formula for this is:

> **Percentage of Workload Needing Average Contribution – (minus) Percentage of Individual Input Required = (equals) Final Outside Team Resource Commitments Needed**

The Final Outside Team Resource Commitments Needed percentage in this example is 55%. This is a workable number as it is not more than twice the Percentage of Individual Input Required, added to the Percentage of Individual Input Required. At any percentage above 60% as the Final Outside Team Resource Commitments Needed (given that the Percentage of Individual Input Required is 20%) this project would require more than double a normal workload for any given team mate and could not sustain the effort resources needed.

Table 4. Effort Expectancy Index

Time Requirement Index Number	Final Productivity Norm Index Number	Final Outside Team Resource Commitments Needed	Effort Expectancy Index
75 minutes (1.25 hours)	10	55%	55% (Final Outside Team Resource Commitments Needed) x (multiplied by) 10 (Final Productivity Norm Index Number) = (equals) 5.5 **(55% x 10= 5.5)** ÷ (divided by) 1.25 hours (Time Requirement Index Number) = (equals) **4.4** **(5.5 ÷ 1.25=4.4)**

The Effort Expectancy Index provides a number, based on the previous three tables' final outputs, used to decide the viability of a team project. An Effort Expectancy Index number between one and five (1-5) indicates a team project workable with current resource inputs. If the Effort Expectancy Index number is higher than five then the team project needs to be re-evaluated for resource needs, workable goals, and deliverable expectancies.

The team project specifications used in the effort expectancy tables provided in the examples show a team project that is on target to complete team goals and fulfill the team purpose. These figures also show that it is possible for this team project to create a return on investment (ROI) over and above simply meeting team goals. The Effort Expectancy Index above indicates the team purpose is beneficial to meeting the mark of reasonable achievement within production status quo. The formula for calculating the Effort Expectancy Index is:

Final Outside Team Resource Commitments Needed (from Table 3.) x (multiplied by) Final Productivity Norm Index Number (from Table 2.)

÷(divided by)   Time Requirement Index Number (from Table 1.) =

(equals) Effort Expectancy Index

Purposing a team project, in a realistic way through measurable potentials in effort expectancy, allows a team to consider how "More" can be achieved and the resources and team goals that will best uphold and contribute to "More" than just working to a set of deliverables. Determining goals is another set of exercises and concepts that enforce the need for Purposing correctly and material on "Goals" is explored in the next section along with the Principles of Competition. The TEAM(work) concepts of "Together", "Everyone", "Achieves", (when actively implemented by a team structure), allow for the potential of "More" to become a definitive productivity contributing to success. In the next half of the book, the model for "**T**ogether **E**veryone **A**chieves **M**ore" will add the implications of "work" for a thorough look at other elements that arise in the TEAM environment.

Goals

Goals are not simply one type of statements setting the bar for achievements. Various types of goals exist. Goal types include: absolute goals; intermediate goals; recovery goals; and external goals. When a team comes together to state their purpose and put goal in place, consideration must be given to more planning than only creating flat determinations of failure and success.

Absolute goals state both purpose and finality and retain the highest mark for team success measurements. An absolute goal achieved decides the endpoint of a team function. Completing absolute goals requires re-teaming for other purposes.

In examining intermediate goals, teams acknowledge crucial pivotal criterion. Intermediate goals are not goals determined in the middle of a project and are not goals that mark the halfway point toward completing absolute goals. Intermediate goals pivot the team progress upward or downward. For example: The absolute goals for TEAM X included the goal of re-establishing financial independence for a departmental product. At the beginning of their project, TEAM X set milestone goals in their planning to benchmark progress. When management examined the history of the project, at the end of the project it was apparent that not all of the benchmarks were intermediate goals. One of the milestone goals set by TEAM X in planning included establishing a budget for the product rollout. This was not an intermediate goal because product rollout did not form a direct corollary to sustained consumer financial support. Another milestone goal had been set in planning for implementing new product improvements to the product design. This was an intermediate goal because new product improvement directly impacted consumers' decisions to support or reject the product and the product's use. The absolute goal of re-establishing financial independence for the departmental product relied on the success or failure of the intermediate goal to implement improvements to the product. Achieving the intermediate goal led to progress toward the absolute goal. Failures of the intermediate goal created a downward turn in the project's sustainability.

Recovery goals are not goals set for achievements. On the other hand, recovery goals are more than just contingency plans for failures. Having a set of recovery goals in place before a team need arises is counterproductive and creates an alternative set of goals to the team purpose that may be considered as acceptable decisions. A recovery goal is not set until there is a team project need to either bring workload progress in line with expectations or to take the team project resource commitments in a different direction. Failure may not have occurred yet, but recovery goals may be needed to avoid failures. To set a recovery goal, a team must show how the recovery goal contributes to the team purpose and will align resources and benchmarks with intermediate goals.

At times, recovery goals can also be external goals. External goals use resources outside of the team resources and incorporate input from external work not included in team planning or team commitments. Recovery goals are not necessarily external goals and external goals are not necessarily recovery goals. A team requirement for external resources or external work input can be an added effort to achieve "More" or part of the necessary effort expectancy planned at the beginning of a team project.

Competition

Teams compete in the marketplace against rivals, internally against each other, and against the established status quo to break new ground with higher achievements. The mentality of competition is crucial to financial gains and progressive advancement of new returns on investments. Competition is viability, but the focus of competition can undermine the foundation of higher standards and fair distributions.

There are two different ideologies capable of fostering competition. The first school of thought focuses on "whose better, whose better, whose best". Teams engaging in this type of competition are encouraged to beat out each other and the focus is on perfective tendencies. Focus falls from the purpose of the team goals, the work to achieve to a higher standard, and the "bigger picture" of how the team fits in the community. Instead, in this first type of competition strategy, the team turns to damaging behaviors that produce less returns such as: achievements to uphold the team's reputation, setting team standards for others, and team centric team mates. Narrow scope of vision can result from one-upmanship and the inability to admit to failures leads to unfulfilled commitments that cannot be worked out through team project processes.

The second type of competition ideology embraces closely the attributes found when the concepts for "**T**ogether **E**veryone **A**chieves **M**ore" are in place. Competition in a TEAM(work) team creates a hunger that drives work, feeds initiative, and creates synergies and motivations that increase with successes. This is a corrected type of competition ideology that increases gains with each achievement, instead of decreasing value, worth and resources. Leadership mentality develops the idea of competition as non-divisive and fosters an environment where failure is not a concept to defeat, but instead failure is just a non-option. In this concept of competition, popularity is never a focus and the "top and bottom" state of mind is replaced by team orientation toward achievements and realization.

Some of the team elements directly impacted by competition ideology include: team purpose; team goals; process execution; standards applications; team cohesiveness and synergies; and motivation and initiative. Competition will arise in any team effort where results are expected. Teams dedicated to their purpose find the realization of their goals.

Exercise B.1.a

Allow as much time as necessary for this Exercise.

Splint the group into two teams. Mark a line on the floor with making tape. (Leave room to stand twelve feet back from the line.) Hand out five sheets of paper to both teams. Explain to the teams the following:

1. They are to create a paper airplane.

2. Everyone on each team must sign their name on the paper airplane

3. Once each team builds their airplane, they must stand twelve feet back from the masking tape mark and fly their airplane over the mark to "finish" the Exercise.

4. This is a competition. The team that finishes first wins.

If someone complains that no one on their team can build a paper airplane, have printed simple instructions (download from the internet) available and pass out a copy of the instructions to both teams.

Once a team wins the Exercise, take a break for ten minutes and then regroup. After the group comes back together hand out a piece of paper and pen to each individual in the group. Ask everyone to individually write ONE good OR bad decision their team made for each element of "**T**ogether **E**veryone **A**chieves **M**ore". (One item for "Together", one item for "Everyone", etc.) Give the group twenty minutes to complete this part of the Exercise and do not let individuals collaborate on their answers. Collect the sheets of paper and open a discussion on how the elements of "**T**ogether **E**veryone **A**chieves **M**ore" affected the goals of the Exercise and the competition environment.

TEAM Image

A team image is the reflection of a team's personality, persona and public presence. When a team has strong leadership team image can be mistaken for these elements of team individuals. Individual images DO NOT create the team image. There is a decisive advantage to not incorporating individual personal elements into team image building. For example: A company requires uniforms with the company logo on them during the work day and usually requests that employees do not wear the company clothing during personal time away from their job. This prevents unpleasant mistakes on the part of non-company members misinterpreting company endorsed behaviors and causes that are the personal freedom of employees on their own time. Team images are similar and should be built carefully and purposely and not simply established due to team mate characteristics. Team image is formed on team time. Associations are human and they create confusion when people stand out as individuals separate from incorporated images that include their own. It is important, for this reason not to single out team mates as characteristic of the team image or to put forward individual team mates in front of the team. Part of understanding a good TEAM(work) concept is acknowledging that the team is composed of individuals and is not an individual effort.

To build a team image, a team can start with what it means to be on the team during the time spent working on any effort toward the team purpose. Focus is on what the team is established for and the team contributions and how those contributions are made. This takes the focus off of individual "star power" and lifts up the TEAM(work) in progress.

Results and the Four R's

Teams are formed to produce results for an end goal or goals according to a comprehensive team purpose. Forming a team requires an established purpose that may or may not be created prior to assembling team membership. Team charters and project planning are beginning steps toward setting team goals that team mates contribute toward taking individual skill sets and attributes into consideration. Meeting goals is not determined by finding the answers to a set of problems in order to obtain credit. Flexibility is a key concept in opening opportunities without the qualification stigma of "pass or fail" team project targets. This does not mean that results are not measurable achievements that complete team purpose fulfillment. Results are team products and achievements that are not based on popular vote, accomplishment inequalities or contributions that do not rise to potential. To differentiate between contributions, accomplishments and results the Four R's (Responsibility, Respect, Resiliency and Reactivity) can be applied to show how each category integrates into team structure parameters. Contributions do not attain to completion and while they may apply responsibility and respect, the end product is not yet achieved. Accomplishments overcome barriers and offer resolution solutions reflected in resiliency and reactivity, but accomplishments are largely not due to existing responsibility and will not normally stand without some sort of imbalance in contributions. Results encompass all of the Four R's and are inclusive of all contributions and achievements. Further, results do not stand without measurable attainments that employ the full potential of the team.

Exercise B.1.b

<u>Materials needed</u>:

- Washable Finger-paints (three colors)
- Whole potatoes (2 less than number of group members)
- Three large baskets
- Stopwatch
- Coin

Split the team into two groups. Give one group finger-paints. Instruct the group with finger-paints to leave the room for twenty minutes and decide on markings for their cheeks (using the finger-paints) as a group symbol. They have the twenty minutes to come up with color choices, type of markings, etc. and must come back with all group members wearing some sort of painting on the cheek(s).

When the group that left the room comes back, have them sit at the tables and give instructions to both groups for the exercise.

<u>Exercise:</u>

1. Flip the coin and have the group without finger-paint markings call "heads" or "tails". "Heads" will go first.
2. Instruct the group going first to remove half of the potatoes from the full basket of potatoes to one of the empty baskets. Every member of the group must touch at least two potatoes during the transfer. Start the stopwatch and time the exercise.
3. Record the time it takes the group to complete the task.

TEAM(work)

4. Have the second group remove the rest of the potatoes to the second empty basket. Every member of the group must touch at least tow potatoes during the transfer. Time the second group with the stopwatch as well.

5. Put both groups completion time up on a chalkboard or flip chart for the entire team to see.

Start a discussion: (This is a discussion exercise, not a definitive lesson.)

- Did the group with finger-paint feel differently about an effort together than the group without finger-paint?

- Was this a results based task? (Discuss the Four R's-Responsibility, Respect, Resiliency, and Reactivity- and if they are applicable?

- Why did one team finish faster?

Deliverables, Consumables and Resources

Once a team purpose is established, the deliverables of the team goals have to be determined. Team resources and consumables are the bedrock of team efforts toward achievements and should be identified and quantified before attempting to establish deliverables. Deliverables are not team goals; they are the products produced by team achievements that fulfill team goals. Resources and consumables can be identified as internal or external and should include both hard and soft assets.

Resources are reservoirs that provide certain needs to the team goals (rather like drawing water from a well- the resource is the well not the water). Consumables can be identified as the inputs used that will not be renewed without a resource and that can be expended. (A consumable would be the water from the well.)

When considering resources and consumables, each input requires evaluation for use, position establishment, and assessment of potential tangible and intangible benefits in regard to expected or required deliverables. If deliverables are decided before consideration of resources and consumables, team planning may find that external or outside additional resources and consumables are necessary.

Determining deliverables following the evaluation for use, position establishment and assessment of benefits for resource and consumable can create more potential for creative internal team decisions. Deliverables should be set after team goals are in place. The idea is not to create a "widget" (deliverable) and then decide how to use it (establish a goal), but to know ahead of time the need to fill (goal) and create the appropriate "widget".

Evaluation for Use

To have a deliverable (output) a team must use resources and consumables (inputs) and perform the work processes (creation) necessary to make the best use of the inputs to arrive at the most desirable outputs to determine proper resource and consumable inputs for the work processes, existing resource and consumables must be evaluated for potential use. This type of evaluation does not reflect the needs for external inputs or resources and consumables that must be acquired. The evaluation for use of resources and consumables should stop short in the evaluation process of assessments for other resource needs.

For example: I have one shoelace and I will need another shoelace to be capable of tying my shoes. (This is not a proper evaluation of the one shoelace already obtained. This statement is an assessment of purpose needs (requirements for shoe tying) instead of an evaluation of the shoelace (width, strength of material, possible variations on functionality, etc.)

There are several reasons for evaluating inputs for use:

1) Assessing properties and characteristics can reveal new potentials and indicate functionality

2) Inventory of amounts and expected resource or consumable life-spans can help determine project time tables and deliverable durations

3) Testing resources and consumables can reveal weaknesses that may affect the deliverable expectations and help to eliminate inputs that cannot be used for the project purposes. Inputs should be evaluated for use before a team project is launched as a preliminary preparation to involving TEAM(work) and can be

performed with or without involving teammates in the process by individuals whom are internal or external to the team membership.

Position Establishment

Position needs to be established for resources and consumables. This entails setting up levels of importance of each resource and consumable to the team project, deciding the order of use required, and creating a "chain of access" for users to acquire, requisition or borrow needed inputs. Creating a position for each individual resource and consumable diminishes the need for team mates to have personal position in relation to team contributions. Team mates that appropriate resources and consumables for their own can become problematic in denying the team inputs needed as they are needed. When position is established for resources and consumables the timetable for input needs and the accesses required to obtain them are already in place. Although individual team mates may be responsible for obtaining or supplying certain inputs, there is not availability to express inappropriate ownership which can impede team achievements. Resource and consumable position criteria should take into consideration the number of team mates requiring use, the frequency of team use and the duration of use. Positions for inputs may change throughout the course of a team project. Team project planning is adaptable, and although resource and consumable position establishment should occur at the beginning of team project planning, input position establishment should be flexible enough to meet changing team project parameters. Declaring specific resources and consumables "off limits" except to predetermined team mates is not a best practice and can also harm the idea of working together in the team environment. This does not negate personal responsibility for the use of inputs and the production of outputs or the designation of individual roles for specific functions. Teams that have team mates that are divisive or unsupportive of one another have individuals and sub-groups that begin to eliminate individual roles and functions of other team mates. This can be a cause or effect that leads to access restrictions of resources and consumables. There is a section later in this book that explores "Team Break Downs (Failures)".

Exercise B.2.a

Items needed for this exercise:

>1/2 yellow crayon
>1 blue crayon
>1 1/2 red crayons
>blank paper
>diagram of a color wheel
>Scotch tape

Lay the items for the exercise out on the table. Explain that the team will have to re-draw a replica of the color wheel with the resources on the table. Ask the team to put a planning document in place that includes an evaluation of the inputs available and determines positioning for the inputs in the plan. Give them thirty minutes to conduct their planning session.

Let the team take a five-minute break. During the break remove the red crayon and half of the blue crayon. (Break the blue crayon in half). Add more blank paper to the "Available" pile. Ask the team to draw up another planning document with the same instructions. Give them twenty minutes.

Tell the team to take another five-minute break. During the second break, add the red crayon and the missing half of the blue crayon back to the table. Remove the paper. Ask the team to draw up another planning document with the same instructions. Give them fifteen minutes.

Take a last break for ten minutes and make enough copies of each planning document for every team member to have one copy of each plan. Ask the team to evaluate the planning documents and choose the most successful prospect for completing the task of drawing a replica of the color wheel. Open up a discussion as to why choose one plan over another. Ask if the evaluations and positioning decisions have affected the planning.

Potential Benefits Assessments (Tangible and Intangible)

Every team and team project has a purpose. Most teams develop goals to attain the team purpose. Part of meeting goals is producing end product deliverables. Potential benefits from deliverables can be both tangible and intangible. When setting the team purpose, potential benefit assessments of tangible and intangible expected future deliverables assists a team in deciding on a direction for achievements. Deliverable benefits can be direct or residual and may be internal or external to the team.

To effectively evaluate potential benefits from team end products, the Five W's of journalism (Who, What, Why, Where and When) can be used to define the expectations of anticipated deliverables. Usually, there will be more than one benefit derived from any given team end product. Narrow scope deliverables may seem like easier outputs to assess, but the task of conducting benefits assessments is actually more difficult when an end product use is limited. Potential benefits assessments are encouraged over actual benefits assessments as proving benefits of end-products requires work past the completion of deliverables under the team purpose Actual benefits assessments demands a new team purpose and re-teaming to follow deliverables and the use of the end-products in post-production evaluations.

Team project deliverables that are perceived as benefits to start with still require an assessment of the perceived benefits of the benefit. The same assessment questions apply to most deliverables regardless of the category of end product. Creating an assessment tool for potential benefits can be a team endeavor and the assessment tool should include the following categories:

- Tangible and intangible aspects of the deliverable
- Internal team impacts of the deliverable
- External customer potential uses and "fallout" impacts of the deliverable
- Narrow and wide scope (little and big picture) indications
- List or number of deliverable customers/uses

The Five W's do not have to be applied to every category used in the team benefits assessments tool, but there should be an answer to each of the Five W's for each team end product by the time benefits assessments are completed.

Benefits assessments are not well used after an end product is completed. Performing benefits assessments gives team leverage for the team purpose or selling power to an external customer. While the timing of benefits assessments can be set at any point during a team project, waiting until a deliverable is finished to conduct potential benefits analyses loses team mobility and flexibility during end product development.

If all team mates are involved in potential benefits assessments for deliverables, then together the TEAM achieves more simply by incorporating broader views on end product uses and assets. Some teams may elect to include the customers for the deliverables in the benefits assessments process as well. Including deliverable customers in benefits assessments encourages team direction toward end product customer satisfaction. The actual benefits assessments process can be tailored for team personality and results.

Team Dynamics

Dynamics are the forces that interact with one another outside the system requirements for a functioning unit. In the terminology of "Team Dynamics" this chapter does not reference the individual composition of interpersonal interactions on a team or the intermingling and combinations of small groups within a larger team structure. Team dynamics refers to the composition of the team as a whole, team positioning within the framework of how a team is structured, and the supports for a team that are external. In other words, team dynamics is inclusive of an entire team and the interactions of the whole team unit as a single structure with those outside the team.

Team dynamics are differentiated by larger and smaller team size impacts and structures and through the concepts of integrated and non-integrated teams. To discuss how teams function as a unit within their environments, some thought has to be given to how the team unit is structured. Once team structures are accounted for, the external environment becomes a foil for team feedback in a didactic system that can influence team behaviors. Individual team composition, or membership, may reflect external team environment influences and resources, but the value of team positioning and structure will change this influence into a separate unit that must function with outside supports in a dynamic relationship once the team is established. An all-encompassing evaluation of team dynamics is not possible due to the interaction of individuals apart from the team unit structure. However, team factors (not individual characteristics) affecting team unit capabilities can be examined for different types of influences on team dynamics.

Integrated and Non-Integrated Teams

One enormous factor in team dynamics is the structure of individual integration within the team. Teams can be structured to function in both integrated and non-integrated patterns. At times, teams will break into smaller units within the team structure and some of these units will only function for team goals in internal team roles while other units will function to obtain team goals using external supports and communications. While exploring this type of team structure is outside the scope of a discussion of team dynamics in this chapter, it is important to realize that this can cause a difference in team integration models by creating a half-integrated/half-non-integrated type of team structure.

An example of a less integrated team structure is a cross-functional team composition. On a cross-functional team, team mates are recruited from other dissimilar teams and skill sets and team functions are sharply delineated in differences on an individual level. With cross-functional teams team mates carry individual skills and functions valuable as non-definable in other team members. Integrated teams often function with similar individual skill sets among team mates and can replace individuals fulfilling team functions with other team mates without too much upset in the team balance. The differences between cross-functional team structures and more integrated team structures affect the positioning and support systems in team dynamics.

Team positioning can affect how a team relates to others outside the team. Different team functions have external support requirements to fulfill team goals.

For example: A team treasurer probably does not require influences outside the team to produce balanced funding for the team. A team management liaison necessarily relays and relies on management support and initiatives to help strengthen team goals. A public relations team officer may not need outside support to fulfill the public relations function, but will depend heavily on outside team influences to guide public relations efforts for effective communications. An integrated team will not have point people in these roles. Integrated teams expect communications with people outside the team to be an open-ended endeavor. On less integrated teams functions necessarily dictate certain team members are responsible for outside team communications in specific areas or roles. Individual team mate communications are still considered team efforts on non-integrated teams with a key concept being free flowing information back to all team mates.

TEAM(work)

Exercise B.3.a

Create two sets of five job descriptions (make both sets identical) on index cards:

1) Treasurer

2) Secretary

3) Public Relations

4) Manager

5) Statistical Analyst

List ONE simple task to be completed for each job description on the cards.

Examples: File reports, add up team dues, pitch project information, etc. Put these tasks on the respective index cards or list them on a blackboard.

Split the team up into two groups. Tell group "A" that the entire group is responsible for all job functions of the group. Explain to group "B" that everyone in the group has to fulfill a different job function. Hand out one set of index cards to both groups. Give both groups the task of answering How, Who, What, When and Where descriptions for all five tasks. Allow 30 minutes for planning for both groups. (Let them plan on their own, individually.) Set up an analysis of the group task question answers.

Large and Small Teams

Team size, or number of team mates, influences team dynamics. Smaller teams operate under efficiencies using multiple role functions according to the team purpose and team goals. Larger teams specify more permanent role functions and rely on cross-functional team member compositions rather than cross-purposing individuals. This affects the manner of interaction team mates conduct with others outside of the team environment. With cross-purposed team mates, most team mates can be approached for any answer needed from the team for those outside the team. In a cross-functional team environment, specific team mates are needed to address differentiated requests originated from the external environment. Integration is a difficult concept on larger teams and an almost ignored element on smaller teams. The difference between integration and non-integration of team mates is reliant on the factors of communication, structure dependencies, and development methodologies.

For example: On Team A, weekly meetings are held for team coordination, but team mates 1 and 2 must finish their work before team mates 3 and 4 can begin their contributions. On Team B, weekly meetings are held for product coordination and team mates 1 and 2 work closely with team mate 3 and 4 so that all work on the product is finished simultaneously. The question of integration or non-integration should not be confused with a business culture. Regardless of size and numbers or team structures, an open business culture leaves room for any question from any team mate to be asked and addressed by any individual. In a closed business culture, team mates are restricted to team purpose and goal oriented communication and individuals are not encouraged to answer questions without assurances about the information.

Exercise B.3.b

Divide the team into two equal groups. (If there is an odd number then put an extra person on either team.)

<u>Items needed</u>: 2 rubber balls

        Pens or pencils

        Paper

Keep the instructions for each group secret from the opposite group.

Group "A "is to assign every group member a different role and function.

Group "B" is allowed to assign group members functions, does not have to assign functions and roles, and may use as many group members in the same role or functions as the group members like.

Tell both groups that they will have twenty minutes to plan. The objective of the planning is to accomplish the following goal: Devise a method of bouncing a rubber ball in such a way that every group member only touches the ball once and the ball only bounces once between each pass to another group member.

Give both groups twenty minutes of planning time. When the twenty minutes is up Group "A" will explain their plan to Group "B "and Group "B" will execute Group "A's" plan. Then Group "B" will explain their plan to Group "A" and Group "A" will execute Group "B's" plan.

Once both plans are executed reveal the different beginning instructions to both groups.

- Did Group "A" or Group "B "show more, (or less), integration?
- How did the group team dynamics affect the execution of the planning by the opposite group?
- If there was an extra person in one group then how did this affect the group planning?
- Could the planning by either group be improved?

Exercises for the rest of the topics discussed in this book are not available as practicing for Failure and related problem solving resolutions is antithesis to the concepts in Together Everyone Achieves More.

Team Break Downs (Failures)

Unfortunately, not every team succeeds in their endeavors to work together to achieve more. Addressing team failures requires focusing on problem solving and resolutions. It is important to start out a new team with a positive mindset geared toward success without focusing on potential failures. On the other hand, when a team faces a break down in forward motion toward goal achievements, it is also necessary to evaluate stumbling blocks in order to arrive at solutions that will enable team mates to recover from set backs. Barriers to achieving more together include internal team elements such as: inappropriate goal setting, excessive consummation of resources, lack of cohesive integration, and team structure inadequacies. External elements such as: resource limitations, customer relations to team dynamics, competition, and the invalidation of team purpose are outside the scope of control and adaptation for solutions originating at the team level.

Team management relies on defining and conducting operations for team supports, structure, and positioning. When there is a team break down these three areas of team management can be crucial to restoring team functions. Team building is not only dependent on team mate communication and contributions, successful teams are managed successfully. With the concepts outlined in this book for TEAM(work), a foundation can be created for variations within team structures appropriate for the internal and external team environments. Using the TEAM(work) concepts does not guarantee team success. On the other hand, the TEAM(work) model is a tool to use to produce better results and decisions for achieving more together. This does not imply that the TEAM(work) model is meant solely for management implementation. Due to the understanding that full participation and team success depends on the entire team embracing the concepts and structures that uphold the team environment capabilities to contribute well in team roles and functions are strengthened by sharing in the knowledge base of TEAM(work).

Problem Solving

When teams run into problems and issues there is usually an effort to resolve, counteract or change troubling situation. Systems such as Root Cause Analysis and Process Purging along with improvement initiatives such as Brainstorming and Statistical Analysis are common methods of attacking problems.

Simplifying the equation: Problem Solving= Problem Identification + Change Analysis x Resolution Implementation

The different approaches toward fixing failures still require every piece of the Problem Solving equation to succeed. Although there are more accepted and prescribed methods for working through solving failure problems,, understanding the basic Problem Solving equation leaves room for innovation and adaptations in problem solving methods that can still be validated across most business relationships,

In relation to team failures, (because each team structure has unique purposes and goals and is composed of varying individual skill sets), the Problem Solving equation becomes important as a basis to form the use of tools and processes already within the team's resources to address working improvements to prevent failures from becoming team eliminations. There should not be one team leader or manager that cannot grasp the basic Problem Solving equation for working to help team mates unless there are other breakdowns in communication and understanding.

Problem solving is sometimes mistakenly thought of as part of the PDCA cycle and is truly different than the scope of just implementing Continual Improvements. It is specifically meant to address failures and issues that have become stop blocks to progress "as planned" or "as usual". Problem solving should always be a reaction to failure. Team's that quit or give up on their goals or purposes without attempting any problem solving show that they never teamed successfully in the first place and that there has been no serious team commitment toward achieving more.

TEAM Punishment

The propensity of team mates to take out frustrations on one another and penalize faults and failure results with team mate punishment is a large part of human nature that varies across the human composition of team membership. Part of determining the appropriate response to team mates in attempts to regulate behavior with consequences requires a mechanism in place for meting out authority; deciding allotments of credits and blames; and proposals and acceptances of measures of restrictions and limitations or payment in order to adjust team punishments. Teams functioning together in proper TEAM(work) principles should construct their own mechanisms and processes for team punishments. Not all teams are built for complete individual team mate inputs into building team punishment structures. On the other hand, (according to the concepts included in the concepts of "**T**ogether **E**veryone **A**chieves **M**ore"), team members should agree to the planning established providing framework and determinations for team punishment regulations. Also, in some team structures team leads or management can add-in ways to mitigate consequences and avoid starting within the processes built to correct team mate behaviors and interactions that cause unnecessary damage to the team or other team members.

Team punishment is not implemented for damage recoveries of resources or inputs without causing a cessation of the causes and effects in motion that have created the needs for team punishments. When punishment is implemented with success, detrimental team behaviors stop. Other team interactions must be established to maintain the functions affected by the eliminations enforced in punishments.

Directing characteristic team interactions in different flows and inventing new uses for skills and resource implementations can create a better team environment after effective team punishment as well as building and establishing new team methodologies and goals. Team punishments are not intended harmful to teams or team members, as the purposes of team punishments are to end team damages. Punishments used from outside the team structures are not team punishments. When stronger authorities and restrictions outside the team structures are necessary to enact team punishments, TEAM(work) has already failed to such an extent that the team is no longer functional as a unit. At this point, team punishment is futile and the only two reasons for following through on team punishments are: 1) To disband team mates refusing to acknowledge team failure; and 2) To control damages and stop team influences reaching beyond the team still reliant on team resources and team inputs.

Recovery

The concept of recovery applies to regaining anything lost. When recovery is applied to a team situation, several types of implementations may be required to keep the team together. Categories included in team recovery processes include: resource and support recoveries, team cohesiveness and function recoveries, and direction, goal, and planning recoveries. Team replacements and re-teaming are two important key recovery oriented cornerstones necessary to teams that will not continue to remain when the situational breakdowns for the team environment result in needs failing under other recovery methods.

Recovery actions are not always completely successful. Although the goal of well-crafted recovery measures is to obtain comparable or more than the losses of any restoration targeted in recoveries, returns on recovery measures may be null, partial, or full successes. The reasons for planning and creating team recovery processes and functions is encompassed in the acknowledgement of the reality of team failures. When a team experiences a type of failure it is not requisite to immediately determine that the team is no longer functional and should not remain a team. Implementing team recoveries is a beneficial decision prior to determining team disbandment.

Outside resources and input may be solicited to enact and facilitate recovery measure requirements. Non-team contributions to recoveries are considered outside sourcing. Control of outside input to team recovery processes and measures (which should already be in place) is either included in established team recovery planning, team leader or team management decisions at the time recoveries are required, or a team decision about terms demanded from outside contributors that will or will not enable outside resources.

Replacing TEAM mates

In recovery measures, team resources remaining in any form should not be cut to perform team repairs. Once recovery processes are exhausted, replacing team-mates by elimination and replenishing functional capabilities for the missing resource input from team mates eliminated becomes the most preferred next option for successful team repurposing. Replacing TEAM-mates is not an easy decision and should not be based on a resource conservation, duplication or advantage increase due to upgraded resource potential in a functional replacement. This is due to the fact that Replacing TEAM mates is due to recovery failure in team resource losses and other reasons for TEAM mate replacements is an admission to a failed team structured from the beginning of teaming. Team goals and resources, including team mate roles and role functions, can be re-evaluated for better team success in team product. This is not the same as destroying the concepts of teaming in Together Everyone Achieves More by rearranging team structures for better resource use. Team mate retentions are crucial in every concept to maintain a valid team has not ceased.

Selection processes for team mate functions and resource replacements should include all team members remaining in the input factors before the final resource replacement decisions. Determinations cannot be suspended for team mate replacement decisions due to input gathering and analysis. Team mates remaining should have an opportunity to contribute the appropriate level of input the team structure allows or the situation resulting in team mate resource replacement requires. Situational requirement restrictions are limitations on decisions without appropriate remaining team mate input. Situational restrictions do not need to be complicated by further restrictive decision making and creating process implementations. Team mates remaining given the opportunity to contribute to input for team mate functions and resource replacement due to team mate eliminations cannot be demanded to respond and should have limitations on their refusals for input by process and team remaining structures.

Reteaming

Reteaming is a choice after entire team failure, including recovery measures and attempts at replacing team mates have been assessed and rendered correctly ineffective. In order to reteam, an acknowledgement of team failure and denial of existing team remaining is required. The concept of reteaming encompasses the understanding that team cessation can reincorporate elements of a team separated when team failure is determined complete. To reteam is to create a new team concept that denies previous teaming to reteam.

When reteaming training team mates and determining resource use and goal sets should not incorporate devaluing the previous team experience. Reteaming requires that team mates and resources bring their full current value to the needs of the new team created. Acknowledgement of previous team experience and value is necessary and should not be required team mate denials for new team values or the reteaming for renewed purposes and goals. If denials of previous teaming are required the values of experience and learning are denied. Knowledge gained and resources acquired that value in team mates reteamed will be limited by requirements that will not value correctly for new team returns and success.

Evaluations for previous team mate resources incorporated in a reteaming effort demand individual honesty and value assessment for reteaming required for the new team's purposes. Team failures that result in team cessation after all recovery efforts are reasonably expended should not penalize individual team mates as the previous team is no longer a standard. Past team mates reteamed from old teaming that has failed have to embrace reteaming is not reassembling old team goals, purposes and synergies. This capability determined is crucial to the assessment of failed teams resources successful incorporation in reteaming efforts. Assessments of reclaimed team mates and team resources for reteaming should never be used in a way that harms the remaining team mate and team resource values retained.

Appendix

Optional Exercise 1

"The Nature Walk"

Split the team into two separate groups. Supply one group with a large garbage bag full of paper scraps. Tell both groups they are going to take a "Nature Walk" today. (Have a non-industrial area outside of at least 1 mile available to walk.)

Instruct the group with the garbage bags full of paper scraps to leave all the paper along the trail during their walk. Start them on their walk twenty minutes ahead of the group without garbage bags with paper scraps.

Supply every member of the second group with empty small individual trash bags. Instruct the second group to pick up the paper the first group leaves behind.

Rule: No one may leave the trail specified for the walk.

Objective goal for the first group: Arrive twenty minutes or more ahead of the second group at the end of the walk AND prevent the second group from achieving their goal of collecting all of the paper scraps left behind.

Objective goal for the second group: Arrive at the end of the walk no later than twenty minutes behind the first group's arrival at the end of the walk AND pick up every scrap of paper the first group leaves on the trail.

One group must fail for the other to achieve their objective.

The first point of this exercise is to explore what happens when one team is split into two teams. Discuss how it felt to be in competition against others that were all one team before the groups were divided up.

The second point of this exercised is that, in a work environment, teams will always have to deal with what someone else left behind them. Consider alternative scenarios in a discussion such as: What if the second group had been ahead of the first group without changing team objectives? How many people felt like changing groups? What would have happened if either group had "quit" before finishing the walk? (Did either group quit?)

The third point to this exercise is to show how working together can be difficult when goals are positioned with "win or lose" or "lose and lose" objectives. Talk about how both groups would restructure the goals for a "win and win" Nature Walk.

Optional Exercise 2

"Backward Storming, Forming, and Norming"

The purpose of this Exercise is to show the breakdown in the process of Storming, Forming and Norming when it is used to create standardization.

Give an example: "Jim" manufactures widgets for Company X.

Ask the team to decide on the "normal" characteristics a general manufacturing employee would exhibit on the job. List the characteristics on a blackboard or flip chart.

Once the list is complete, form a profile from the characteristics of Jim and a hypothesize a typical day's routine of forming the "widgets" of Company X. Be sure to include team input in this. Lead the team through the forming stages.

Take a team break for half an hour. While the team is on break, put the profile and Jim's hypothetical "routine day" down on paper and make enough copies for everyone on the team.

When the team returns, had out the profile of Jim and his day. Instruct every team mate to list (on their own page) five elements of the profile that are counterproductive, non-efficient, problem/error causing, etc. (five negative items).

This exercise is Norming, Forming and Storming. Talk to the team about how it is not beneficial to take new ideas and create Norms and standards without looking at the Norms and standards already in place and identifying problem areas. Show them how this exercise was actually thinking in reverse. "Where we are" is identified before addressing the question of "Where we are heading". If the team had been given the list and asked to identify the negative items first, without defining the norms and then examining what they had defined for flaws, then the flaws would be assumed as "externally" applied instead of "internal" to the team's own work. Open up a discussion on how to incorporate this type of Norming, Forming, and Storming to improve team ideas as opposed to "aftermath" evaluations.

Optional Exercise 3

"Apple Slice and Dice"

This Exercise is short and simple.

Divide the team into groups of five people each. If there are "extra" people, have them sit out.

Hand each group an apple and a paring knife. Explain that everyone in the group should be given an equal part of the apple and that no part of the apple can be cut in half more than twice.

Wait to see how each group divides the apples.

Start a discussion about why numbers matter to outcomes. Talk about resource limitations (there is only one apple per group). Did some groups wind up with "more apple" left over? Did any group choose not every group member had a piece of apple? Team resources include that some team mates may have had to "sit out". How does this affect the outcome of apple slice divisions?

Explain the purpose of the Chapter on "More" is to help define questions related to "dividing up apples".